DODGE & BURN

Linda Reardon Neal

BAMBAZ PRESS
Los Angeles 2014

ACKNOWLEDGMENTS

Grateful acknowledgment to the editors of magazines and journals in which some of the poems (or earlier versions of them) in this volume have appeared: *California State Poetry Quarterly; Embers Poetry Journal; Myriad, the Creative Arts Journal of El Camino College; ONTHEBUS; Pacific Coast Journal; Peregrine, the Literary Journal of Amherst Writers & Artists; Poetry Revival, An Anthology from the National Kidney Foundation; Sculpture Gardens Review; Word Gifts, in Celebration of Older Americans.*

Some of the poems first appeared in limited edition chapbooks: *Naming What Remains (2012), Color Bleeding (2012), Without (2013).*

Special Thanks

To my writing buddies over the years — the Salon Marathon men and women, and the Gaman women, the Thursday afternoon group at Jack Grapes' Method Writing class, the members of Deena Metzger's healing and writing community, as well as to Jack and Deena for their generous gifts as mentors and extraordinary human beings, to Denyce Giannioses for her editing and design skills and to Baz Here and Bambi Here of Bambaz Press for their unflagging support.

Cover design by Linda Cotter (with Baz Here)

ISBN: 1499240880

BAMBAZ PRESS
Los Angeles, California USA
Printed in the United States of America

for
Mike

Time keeps on slippin,' slippin, slippin'
Into the future . . .

— Steve Miller
"Fly Like an Eagle"

CONTENTS

Cirrus Wisps

Archaeology

Mistral

Thinking of William Carlos Williams

A Summer or a Season

Sassy Facts

Weeping and Laughter

Cloud Life

CIRRUS WISPS

The Parent of Stories

Poetry
is an embarrassing howl
a wet animal covered with blood
that arrives straight from the womb
of language. It flows into the world
on an ocean of dependency.

Poetry
needs your tongue
to caress it, your lips to surround it
as it sets up its interminable yawp,
hoping you will pay attention
as it twists the buttons off your shirt.

Poetry
knows no shame
as it attempts to come
into your mouth and sings out
about the beauty of bodies
that writhe under the moon.

Poetry
is a bastard,
a skin-hungry orphan
who becomes the parent
of stories told by sad housewives
to their telephones.

Hidden beneath
Poetry's colorful sweater of stones,
you will find Rigoletto's aria
and the chisel of a sculptor
who died
for the certainty of marble.

Cheat Notes

The many return to the one
What does the one return to?
— Zen Koan

Fall blows sand against Dukkha House.
I'm sweating as quiet as cotton.
Autumn. Wind. Curtains flap
my shadow long
upon the cabinet; clothing
hangs in the closet
and I sit, alone,
watching shirts in a closet
watching my self on a cushion,
dividing the parts into doer and watcher.

Pushing into the far desert of mind
past sloppy sentiment,
I'm frozen in the high desert
that speaks of death. Here
      yet again
      curled up, waiting
      to be born from the belly of sand.

And what does the one return to?
The body of the ego is small,
a size five, and I'm back to back
with this self that grows
as bread rises,
back to back with her
again. We sit on the same bed,
in this oven-hot desert.

I dream of India —
of gurus who speak ancient tongues
of squalor and beggars in the street.

If I had a begging bowl I would polish it
with my tongue, and if I said
I was writing this to you
that would be true, but if I told you
this was a tribute to Ruth Denison
that also would be true. If I told you
I was writing it
for no one to hear or to see
would the many return to the one?

Black Rock Principle

—after Georgia O'Keeffe
Black Rock with Blue III

I am black earth mountain body
full round mother of stones.

I know
time and erosion
the slow slippage of sand —
shadows lean on me
and streams bubble over my back.

I've heard night air drip
ether on dust and watched saguaro's transitory bloom.

I've witnessed Lord's Candles glow in yuccas' arms
and the round, lonely moon rise at dusk.

Harsh sunlight greets each day
to teach me about blue sky and heat
and what it is to yearn to sleep
alone, soothed by dark sky.

I am patient with my lessons —
eons have smoothed me.

You will know
when you've become rock.
You'll feel the simple solitude of roundness,
no longer be tempted
to crawl into angled spaces.

Something Has Happened

To Sound this Week.

My phone has stopped

ringing.

My car radio went dead.

I've lost my voice

and

The rain is speaking in sign.

Panache of the Plumeria

Since I'm going to die
I want to do it
with the panache of the plumeria,
all scent and golden form
lunging deeper into the morass
of my leopard thirst for this life
connecting to the electric heart of song
not the beaten-down vibration
of drums on the verge of music, but
of my dog licking my face —
the feel of her tongue as rich as
any lover's scratches, even as I know
the denseness of her tongue won't save me
from sinking past my body.

I empty my yearnings on the dresser
each night, the stones of dreams,
the gold and silver metallurgy of my hopes
landing in small piles, as I toss my desires
onto the pile with every ring.
Each strand of a three-strand silver necklace
each totem on the Inuit bead necklace
becomes a memory of the way my sons laughed
standing knee-deep in long grass on the edge
of the Owens River.

And the river travels on
and down and through the valley
running in every direction
inevitable flood of life
ever-reaching toward its own end
while I stand by, watching the pieces of my body
gather momentum to disappear
into a cover of cirrus wisps
bit by bit

just as sure as I stand by the dresser
and peel the gems and metal off my limbs
one by one
stone by stone
just as sure as day becomes sunset
just as sure as sunrise is a chimera waiting its turn.

Driving Wild

Driving hot coals

        raining
        no —
                landing

                        like hard gems on

asphalt

        no —
              driving cold hail
                    shatters trees

                              I must
                              choose

              Silence
                or
        A mushroom cloud becomes a pet

                  Conversation goes one way —
                        starved
                  she conducts a monologue

I am not there

                    She is a voice from
                      planet loneliness

            These driving words
            This driving life

is not simple
        I think
            a monument to my own lost sensuality
                        a valley
                        a canyon

                                                        The
                                                        flesh
                                                        tears
                                                        first

Then the mind
        spearheaded by tantamount to nothing

                                All that glows is not glitter

Mudflaps on a Model T
Mud hens on a pond
Muddy diagonals streaming
        Rainboots steaming

                        Wilderness is within my reach

ARCHAEOLOGY

Archaeology

I find a stone
place it in the garden
refrain from eyeing it
or carving it
or dreaming jewelry
cut and polished
but go searching for its family
in dry lava flows
turning the rock
into a creature like myself.

In my attempt to honor it
I go about seeking
its origins
in what remains
after floods and fires
in the veins that mark
a mountain's skin.
I follow bloodlines
on the mountain mother
see how they spill down
to become cracks
that split the desert
and make a wilderness of sand.

For just a moment
when it rains
we will move toward each other
and recall who we are.

Wake up Digging

If you had believed in sound
before the silence grew into an ocean
and before I had swum in the warm salt sea
perhaps
I would not have called out with my arms
and heard only the language of rowing.

> There was a time, before the rowing, before
> I saw the old man, when I was inside
> and you put your ear up to her belly
> to hear me swimming there, in that salty ocean
> where the three of us were joined
> until

I clasped my toes in spasm, emerged
woman from woman
from water, and now
waiting to feel you, on shocking summer nights
I wake up
        digging for my father.

Fisherman's Wife

Spring, summer, fall
falling over the river
where I wade,
my camera
around my neck
me at the edge
them in the middle
of the Owens,
thigh-high rubber boots
pushing through the reeds,
father threading flies
for his sons
while ice crackles
on the surface of the water.

In a fall rain, I close my finger
over the shutter,
to catch all three
wade their way upriver
while the cold-blooded browns
shift their way
beneath the surface.

I don't catch fish
just memories
in the box
around my neck,
as the water
the men
the fish, all slip by
until the winter is too deep
the willows too bare for birds.

I walk and wade,
bite pine nuts between my teeth

dip to my knees
to snap a brown
just below the surface,
a rainbow across the sky
my husband's back
as he leads the boys
through the current of reeds.

I'm a fisherman's wife
and these are good days
but cold. I love the boys
even for the ways
they are like their father.

Remains of a Marriage

We stood facing each other
on the stone stairs
of the glass chapel
with its blue steepled arm
reaching into the sky. Stephanotis draped
from my gloved hand
invoking the aroma of sweet possibility.
The Swedenborgian minister read
the marriage rites out loud
and a still space began growing
between my new husband and me,
the only movement a baby
beginning in my belly.

Holding on for years
to black and white photographs
in a white leatherette album
we grappled through disharmony,
on the days when the marriage
was not in question
but, really,
our marriage was always in question.
We stayed together
because neither wanted a divorce
at the same time. Neither wanted a child
at the same time either
so we had two sons.

I can't forget that glassed-in beginning,
or the hideously tasteful finish —
my soon-to-be-ex-husband and his porcine attorney
weighed down with documents in manila folders
as our two family-law specialists faced off
amidst books and leather
and the smell of furniture wax and shoe polish.

Wearing a deep purple shirt-dress, I sat
waiting, in a mahogany chair
until the men
dressed in three-piece grey
paraded through the door
and unloaded stacks of papers
on the polished table in the middle of the room
while a crystal clock in the bookshelf
ticked off what was left of our union.

The Spanish Plate

Still waiting to be chosen,
years after our wedding,
I prayed for one more poem in our feet
just one more spin across the pages
that might have led to the possible book
just one more chance
for our lives to fall between the covers
the way we had dreamed.

Possibility arose in Seville
with the mournful echo of guitar music
in an Andalusian plaza, where
the scent of pomade from a flamenco player's hair
floated midair, and fragile dishes lined up
in a shop window, waiting
like brides, to be chosen.

We selected a plate, a round one, full
of bright blue and yellow flowers
with green tendrils twirling off
the edge. None of it, not the music
not the foreign smells, not the warm breeze
could have predicted the night
when you would claim the plate
while we sat at the kitchen table
drinking red wine, dividing our keepsakes
accompanied by *Concierto d'Aranjuez*
first by Segovia, then by Miles.

I didn't expect to be sitting here

alone

listening to Segovia and Miles
drinking cinnamon-licorice tea

my bathed feet propped on an aged ottoman,
my head still planted
in the remains of our fantasy life.

Body Going Down

My mother flails her arms
the *iv* jitterbugging in her flesh.
and the oxygen tube in her nose
waggles its warning as she roars
"It's hell to die like this, piece by piece!"

The fear that rules her
keeps her from hearing
the COPD diagnosis,
but we both know
she will drown
in her private devil's triangle
to become the bloated manatee
of her nightmares
washed up on the shore
of her unlived life.

Behind the stanchions of her gated garden,
ruled by the tube in her nose
she sits in a wrought iron chair
drawing up a five-year plan —
to plant more berries and pink plumerias,
which dividends to keep, which to reinvest,
and how to worry my brother and me
into her life.

I peek at the lists
when I order our chicken dinner,
and while we wait silent for the delivery,
we pull snails off young strawberry plants
and give them to salt.

She drags herself toward the kitchen
washes snail slime from her fingers
and sets the table for our meal.

We don't talk about hemlock
or coffins, or coffers filled with rue,
and I don't ask her
what she wants of her death —
a box of bones or an urn full of ashes
because we both know
we all end the dance
in a dark container
traveling through unknown dimensions,
feral spirits
becoming nothing nowhere,
if not a sea sponge,
or a hardball with stitched red seams.

Counting Ants

Perhaps there are people
who know how to ask
or even how to receive
so for them
each breath is a gift from god.

But what if you are not one of them?

What if your questions fall
into that impractical silence
that comes
after listening to a brass quartet?

Just now an ant crawled across
the page of this poem,
right through the word
that names him
which leads me back
to the question about god.

How could an ant know
to walk on this poem
and not on any
of the hundred others
 in the stack?
And what is it
about the chalk line I draw
on the brick floor
that keeps ants from crossing over?

I know boundaries
but always circle back
to questions. What comes
after the regular breath of sleep

the copper cavity of dreams
the morphine drip?

Is there a boundary
that separates
the language of dying
from dying
a chalk line around the bed
the room
the family
my mother,
as death enters her aura?

I count ants
on the perimeter of her room
while she is birthed
into that narrow tract
of dust beyond breath.

Tonight
her crone dog
will lead me
to build a ziggurat
to the moon.

Up at 2 a.m.

It's 2 a.m., and I'm up when I should be down
up with nothing to distract me from me
here at the table in the middle of the night
the refrigerator humming, fish smell hovering.

Tonight was the first time I used my mother's blue table cloth
not just any blue, but sapphire blue, bright as the stone in the ring
my father brought back from India, linen embroidery embracing ghosts
of our mother, our father, my brother and me.
We ate when we should have prayed.

Yellow roses in a crystal vase, a few petals on the blue cloth
empty chairs and table; candles stand like sentinels
waiting for the family
that can never be the dream that hovers above the rectangular table
under the lights that make their small hum at 2 a.m.

I pick up a used napkin, blow my nose.
My son's dog sighs. I sigh with him
then rub a rose petal, smooth against my rough skin
watch my hands, empty of the rings that decorate them in daylight,
become my mother's, all knobby and gnarled.

It's 2 a.m., and I am old.
The light from the overhead cans shines down
on my open notebook, as I recall myriad dinners
and dreams of some other family
whose mother didn't slip into a drunken, slurring monologue
whose father didn't go silent after wolfing down his meal
and I remember, too, when

I was wife and mother, setting a table
and cooking a meal for a disparate bunch of relatives
who didn't want to sit together.

The best of times. The worst of times.
It's 2 a.m.
and the rumor of memories sits with me.

Divining Rod

Death is a grounding force
a thing some people would call
a divining rod. It takes you
to your knees, and then
it takes your knees
right out from under you.
Picture the bearded man
in the corner of the alcove
a singular painting
of a gnarled face. No knees.
Just a face, losing itself.

Death comes, that twisted old man
who won't shave his beard
or a bird that mimics
your mother's call
so you won't be afraid
when it's your turn to fly away
break your neck
or wither like a brown leaf.

I sit in the white chair
the one with the seashell pattern
in my living room.
The shells don't move
but sit stationary
under me, at my sides and back
empty boats
that once housed mollusks from the sea.

Death in the corners of the chair.
Death in the photograph.
Death in our family
each one closer than another
first my mother,

now my father
in his Irish green T shirt
and pallid face, every line
that made him real
disappearing on his thready breath.

Now look at me,
taking oranges to the neighbors
because they are a clear sign
that the juice of life is bursting
just beneath the skin
not in the usual places
not my children's eyes,
but in that dark corner
where I set the oranges
this morning
to reflect the sun's light.

I don't look for life
in the old folks' home
the care facility, the hospital
not even the nursery.
I look in my own shirt
that hangs in the closet waiting.
It will outlive me
and it must know that
so crisp and white and clean
on its clear plastic hanger
just the way I hung it there.

And still I lift my heart
to all deaths. I pull my heart
on a string
drag it through the streets
where it can feel all the deaths
that have come before the mollusks
and after
before the horse

that used to pull its wagon up the hill
and after
before the old dog
who dragged herself in and out
of the garden.
I lift my heart to my father
whose rattling breath
leads him out the door
of his mouth.

Silver Windmill

A silver windmill twirls in the naked plumeria tree
shining long rays of light through the window
and across my bedroom wall

I lie here
between these rays

How to make sense of polar opposites
that name so many grand ideas
      war and reparation
      democracy and anarchy
      god and man

Am I foolish to believe
there can be harmony
between the poles?

It would be easy
to love my mother
if we stood
on opposite sides of the garden
each with a silver windmill
in our hand.

MISTRAL

Experience of Bone

The clopping of slow horses   no audible birds
more like Paris than Chicago   at 4am
a banging screen   summer wind cuffing   and sweat
pooling in the middle of the bed   no pills
will stop the trees from walking   or make me sleep
when I'm swollen up like a puffer
gilling my way   to a slow death
at 4am   I am the nightmare   slow-walking
next to the stalking trees   into dawn
in time to grind my own dull march   toward flight
arms flapping   as the daylight storm begins
as just the morning reaches out   from behind
a frenzied scythe of moon

Sinister Swish

Sinister, cryptic, specious, rapacious
the dialysis machine swish, swish sucks
my blood and flushes it back to me
in gestures of generosity, wooshing it through
its make-believe vein in my arm and through my heart,
rinsing. There is no such thing as an easy dialysis date.
It's never the same, and there are always red ants at the picnic
even if I think I am ready for the vomit and blood
the screeching of the machine and the squawking
of the thin grey bird in the next chair.
Or she is me, dripping blood from my arm
vomiting in my lap.

Vomit and blood.
Blood and vomit
and maybe I recover my dizzy self
by the end, stand up straight enough
to fake the composure the nurse demands
to let me walk out the door.

I wave farewell to the twenty other lounge chair tenants
and I wave to the wheelchaired woman in the corner
even pay tribute to that whirring washing machine
that holds "my kidney" in its cold metal arms
as I walk out the door. The nurses are frozen in time
their uniforms as stiff as the words of comfort they offer
one telling me I'm still normal
another chiding me for holding on
to my needlepoint yarn like it's a life preserver.

The acrid smell of dialysate
blood and vomit permeates the brightly lit room
and the moans of the bodies in the chairs
float on the air
as the ambulance attendants remove the woman

who just writhed into a coma-code-blue.
I shut the door behind me and make my way
to the cafeteria to eat the only meal
that won't taste like carbamide
better known as urea, for the next two days.

All the rest will be nausea followed by nausea
followed by sleep. A bright observer
in the cafeteria sees my bulging, bandaged arm and says,
"Isn't it a miracle — dialysis?" I want to stuff him into the oven
or chop off his tongue.

The miracle is that I survive it.
The lights in the cafeteria are too bright.
The floor rises and buckles under my feet
as I take my tray of zucchini and chicken breast
to the linoleum-topped table.

A cup of coffee?
A walnut-studded cookie?
A tomato?
No!

I dream of these forbidden riches.
I want the heavy machinery that binds me to this steely life
to lift me like a bird, a winged overseer, oversoul —
someone who'll lift me from this surreal diorama of days
but there is no door ajar, no exposed cloud
no angel to set me down on a couch of joyous faith
no magic potion, no sereph to twist me
into postures of beauty and release.

My skin is a cold metal wrap
but my feet burn. An icy wind deep inside me
penetrates my frame; my lips crack, and my blood struggles
to be a river instead of a muddy pool in my belly.
The whip of time snaps in my left ear as I set myself down
in a fragile stupor, on the chrome and plastic chair

sure that the witch at the corner table
is cackling a platitude about how lucky I am to be alive
while her dog hunkers outside with his leash wrapped around a pole
where that red white and blue flag of freedom
is flapping its stars in the hot breeze.

After the Transplant

I thought I would be different   I thought
       I would be the same   I thought I would stop thinking
about the transplant   stop dreaming of white rooms   orange juice and
pee
    I would forget about death   filter my life down to what matters
                                sift and name.

    Yet here I am   talking to myself   to everyone
       to this fleshy new being stitched into my belly   He's
memorizing me   I'm learning
what he likes for breakfast   how to pamper him

    Because we are on intimate terms   like any woman with her lover
       any mother with her child   We exchange fluids and feel
our mutual pulse   We sleep together   him just under my skin   and
together
       we've dreamed the surgeon placing him   just so
       lining up the sutures
           molding our fleshes together   giving us to each other
             in this ritual of marriage   in this ritual of
rebirth.

Feng Shui My Way

Death marks the perimeter of my days
even as I point my feet away from the door when I sleep
so people won't mistake me for my corpse.

I hold on to trees, prepare for cleaving
by earthquake, atom bomb, violent conversation at the table
and I speak to the four directions at dawn.

I didn't hang marriage vows in the southwest corner
of the house. We divorced. I didn't place a metal statue
in the window that faces sunrise. I fell ill.

I look in the mirror and see geology, geography
and my biography in lines and a scar as big as a mine field
staked out across my belly.

Must I go west until it is east,
sell my grandmother's Irish linen tablecloth at consignment
teach myself to eat rice instead of potatoes?

Must I use chopsticks and tiny bowls
throw the *I Ching* every morning
move my front door to the south and paint it red?

I have learned to heed the warnings
of the alchemy of air, metal, water, fire, wood
like broken waves in the continuity of music

Coming and going, and like the last three leaves
on the Caribbean Copper tree that cling
to a branch, wagging in the wind.

Each morning I sit, watching my breath,
becoming what I don't understand
in order to give up what I have lost.

Into Pain

Come down
    from that room
        that roof
            that translucent heartbeat

                                backbeat

bite tribal rhythms
                Stick a dog
              in the middle
           of a tambourine riff

It's the same bowl of cherries
           Bing or Frank
              Sing or twinge

      at the thought of your sister, who tries on songs
          like bathrobes.

Every evening wafts
                            the
                  nonsense of the day
                into the cup of my back.

C'mon! What'll it be?
Gimme a break!
Don't waffle.
Just give me the straight scoop.

                I tear off my bracelets.
                Feed them to the dogs
                that howl at the gate

Because

Can you sing?
Like the wind?

We all know the thunder has a song
all it's own:

I'd better never go to Vegas or eat a plantain —
while my back speaks
longitudinal pain
latitudinal ache

Up
Down
Sideways
Inside and upside out

Tell me your pain, Mary Oliver.
I'll scream mine.

I am a walking pain machine

Or a fishing line that only brings in piranhas and pariahs, sea cactus,
and dead men to mourn.

I'm biting my fingertips — better than frostbite, back bite, dog bite
do it myself
to myself
No
part of me
is exempt

My dreams
hide
in nightmares.
Secrets
reside
in
my back
viscious

as
the sky
after a tornado.

She Had Totems
   – after Joy Harjo

She had totems. Elvira Madigan. Mozart.
Teeth and beads. She saved scabs from her sons' knees.
She sucked blood from her sores
and ran her fingers along the gortex shunt
etched in her arm.

She rubbed the lingam stone from the Ganges
petted owl feathers, saved the soft fur
from the underbellies of cats. She saved
gardenia and rose petals
and the bulbs she dug in the fall.
She had totems.

She remembered everything
and collected corn husk dolls, bones
from the Sierra or the Mojave
photographs of cactus and cottonwoods
a tall man and snow.

She had totems.
She ate tubers and sucked the marrow from bones
praying for forgiveness. She saved
blue heron feathers in envelopes
porcupine quills in boxes
pieces of cloth from her graduation and wedding dresses
from her sons' pajamas, from Christo's fence and umbrellas.

She wore silver snakes and lapis on her fingers
and around her neck. She hung an emerald in the window.
She would envy no one. She would tame her greed.
She kept only small mementos: poems by Robinson Jeffers
a box full of sewing needles from her grandmother
and a purple scarf for wrapping the Tarot.
She had totems.

She had her mother's wedding rings converted to gifts
practicing the alchemy of love.

She threw the *I Ching* once a week
whether she needed to or not.
She was not religious.
She was not alone

THINKING OF WILLIAM CARLOS WILLIAMS

Naked, He Calls

Naked, he calls to me
for a bar of soap
revealing his fourteen-year-old
ass and belly
as he flashes
toward the shower.

I wrap this moment
around my heart
because it's all I've got
after a shoelace thin grimace
has wiggled across my face
to tie my lips shut.

I am the genesis
of the first wetness he'll probe
in dreams
because he must —
our lives are sewn together
until he grabs the knife
and cuts.

Cornbread

Tonight I made cornbread the Tassajara way
with a pudding layer in the middle. Tonight
I made cornbread this way for Kevin
Tonight he didn't come home.

When a baby is born, the last thing
you think about is cornbread;
when the baby is sixteen, cornbread
raises its yellow belly, and you know
time has baked wrinkles into your face
just like the map on the surface of the bread.

You look in the mirror, and all you see
is the years, like a dry riverbed,
parched in the California sun,
and you realize you are old enough
to have a son old enough to go away.

You look at the thin skin under your eyes
and the dimples that have become as big as dimes
and you wonder how soup and cornbread
could incapacitate you this way,
paralyze you in your dressing room,
and then you see it's not just your face.

You see how your stomach has etched
its own record of time on its surface.
You see the thick pads beginning
on either side of your waist.
You look at the clothes hanging
in the closet, waiting
for the young woman who won't return.

But you keep your nails neat, find pleasure
in digging in the garden, and you tell your older son

you love him, just like you wish you had
when he was so tiny
he fit in your dresser drawer
and cried in the rocking buggy
in the apartment with the brown formica floor.

So tonight, I eat cornbread and soup
and leave a note for Kevin,
thinking of William Carlos Williams —
that the plums are so sweet   – that this bread is special.
"Butter is fresh from the wrapper,
and honey is in the cupboard."

Tonight I bathe, put on my old, baked skin
and my World Love socks.
I am older than my recipe.

The Fundamental Conundrum

for you, my son

is:

a red pepper   hanging

independent

          of every other question

a poppy reseeding itself
          in the exact spot
          that it must

for the desert to bloom

embracing
          such mystery

                              you place
          the question mark

  in the middle of your life

So Big

Now that you're twenty-three
you wear the irony of the vest
that third piece
pegged across your chest
that locks the key to you
up tight.

It's wrong that you're dressed
so big outside
when inside me
you're still a boy
on war maneuvers —
Bang, Bang —
in the empty lot next door
unaware that your life hangs
by a grey flannel frown.

God, how I wish
you were still three
(for my sake as well as yours)
because if you were only three
there would be so many things
to do different
with you
your brother and your father
and I wouldn't be so full of sorrow
about growing old myself
maybe not care that the older you get,
the older I get.

It's not enough to collect shells and write poems
It's not enough to dream my way back
to those days
when your diapers sagged
with wet beach sand

and I held your hand while you walked
on the ledge along the Strand
the ice plant bank below
the ocean in the distance
and our lives spread out
so big in front of us.

Other Mother's Daughter

His brunet head was once
a heap of straw-blond tangles
and the wet sand stuck between his toes
or weighing down his mini-surfer trunks
reminded me why I never wanted girls
who trap men the way boys catch fish
with a flashing lure.

Some other mother's daughter
will do that and call my son
lover, husband, mate
scratch her ardent fingernails
across his cheek and hip
kiss and feed him right here
in this kitchen where we stand today.

She'll scour out the sink with *bon ami*
and never ask what I cooked for him
or if we stood here then.

I Take My Son to *Les Mis*

In the dim light
of the first row
of the balcony,
I sit making small-talk
with the man
who used to be
my little boy.

He says his black shoes,
the ones
with the tassels,
need a shine
while I sit
smelling his hand
next to me
on the arm
of the chair.

I'm holding a lifetime
in my sweating palms
as I fold my hands
in my lap
and turn my gaze
toward the curtain
as it rises.

Mother, Burning

These lines are for the westering cut cord, coiled in a rich circle
over the small tract of land called my belly
as you swing free from our reptilian dream, and as for me,
pure woman, I'll always be strapped to your sleeping flesh,
ready to smother anything unnatural that rises,
for the wolf that rules me ties me to you, challenges you
to take the blood root that grows from this mother's love
and give it, not to me, but to yourselves.

These lines are not paper page imaginings
but your white teeth shining, your legs growing longer
than your jeans as you walk next to cows in a mountain field
tossing lines toward trout that swim along the bank
bait-knife-reeling yourselves onto manhood
while I watch, walking along the river's edge.

These lines are for dark stairways and wild horses
in cowboy dreams, for allegiance to the rings on tall pines
and your thickening into manhood, ready to come
into your own hands, adult.

These lines are for the finished lessons stored
in moldy closets, garage rafters and attics
for discarded tire pumps and shredded sweaters
sandy days with sunburned cousins
the welcome vinegar rubs that smell like blood
on summered skin, before it peels like paper whites.

These lines are for my greedy envelope of love
the splintered seeds uncovered
for the full apparition of unchained jealousy and longing
sandwiched behind closed doors
between paired gargoyles or avocado halves,
for a mother's love is blind and bleats
like an obsessed dove

but hides in silence underneath the cobra's hood
incandescent, burning for her sons.

A SUMMER OR A SEASON

Trombone in the Garden

Let's not be other people.
Let's stop pretending
we like this hot winter weather
and blondes.
Let's turn out all the lights
and make a fort of desire.
Just this once
let me be the spider.

Or let's pretend
you're a catholic altar boy
and I'm the priest
who gets off
on your embouchure
and delicate slide. Let's bite
walnuts open, shout
hipster vowels, and imagine
we can find the square root of jazz.

The trombone in my garden
is not a peacock, but you
begging my name
my name, my name.

Pulling Music

My lips ache.
I'm the pale shock
you want to believe
the ancient flesh on trees
the voice of the wild dog
from the place of poetry
stretching sound between us.
We pull our music behind.

I'm the carnal opal
as wanton as your songs
my slips falling to the floor
my words dropping off my shoulders
and I'm as weak as my grandmother was
when the Indian twisted her hair
into a knot on the back of her head.
and took her—arms, fingers, lips.

I will crawl to you
like the echo of drums
and howl like a dingo at dawn.
Like my grandmother
who was terrified of the Indian
I will become your hollow horn.
I will adore you.

The Clairvoyant Kiss

Our kisses follow us around
the house, into the bedroom
like black velvet skirts.
Their fuzzy hems
float and rustle
as we breathe.

The first kiss
and the last kiss
and all the kisses
in between

know
who will die
first, and so, who
will be kissing cold lips
under the warm light
of a gibbous moon.

The Vets

They come and go
       They come by car
       They come by bus
       by medical transport
       by wheelchair
They come to the VA limping
pushing walkers
They come and go
on two legs
on stumps of legs
on canes and crutches.

The vets
They come and go
wearing flags around their necks
and they come on gurneys
their bodies wrapped in flags
so I can't tell if they are dead
or alive.

They come
eyes half-closed
mouths gaping open.
Oh how they come and go.

Photographs of recruiters
and eagles, and photographs
of men in starched uniforms and stiff smiles
photographs of helicopters and bombers
line the hospital hallway walls
while the vets
they come and go
and the hallway walls travel
their circles and squares
through catacombs of operating rooms

ultrasounds, endoscopies, colonoscopies
and all the while the eagle rises up
with talons on the roof
and the flags try to flutter
in the hot air
while the vets come and go
through the doors
and down the hallways
where the air is conditional
and they are living the conditions
of the conditioned lives
of their service
to the flag
that strangles them
> or takes their leg
> or their arm
> or their brain.

A woman pushes her man
into the radiology clinic,
checks him in, #4722.
He sits like a statue
mouth gaping, eyes squeezed shut.
She takes out a tissue, dabs
at the ooze from his eyes
then rolls him through the door
pushing him back
> all the way back through battle
> all the way back to Viet Nam
> all the way back into the room.

And the vets, they come and go,
so I look away but only after
a thirty-second stare.
I look away, down at my crossword
and try to think of an eight-letter word
that means eradicated.

A Season or an Appetite

I'm wishing for luck, waiting
for the right combination to roll
that will make Mike all right.
I mean all well, not this dwindle
of brown skin fading to plain
grey hair turning to gauze.

I'm wary and too much aware
of his failure to eat
and I'd like to close my eyes
to the real loss and just sail
into the magazine of the gun
instead
picking through spent shells,

Each one a brass ring
that singes my fingers,
each one burning the truth
of Cupid's blackened darts
into the turquoise stone
on my left ring finger
each one tightening
like the shuttered windows
that wrap around our old house.

I must forget how doors flew open
with abandon, see now
how they bang shut
because summer is only
a season or an appetite.

Pound Every Detail

I don't believe we'll be together
in some better fucking place.

It was this reliable place that was best —
his barbeque, apple pie, Scrabble jive talk.

I fold his baseball caps into shape, hang
them on the hall tree, try to fold my life

into a new shape I cannot fathom and stop wearing
black because my son says, "Mom, that's passé."

I wash his dirty levis, sort his socks
take the silver-green jacket to be laundered

because I want to wear it. Instead I leave it
on its paper-wrapped hanger in the garage.

I swirl dishwater in the sink, play with our toy boats
and rubber duck in the bathtub.

I lift an empty fork to my lips, wear rosemary
on my front door, pin jazz to my lapel,

pull our music through a sieve
rattle my bracelets of rivers and bait a hook for

Nothing.

I lunge because grief is too hot
and cry more than I expected, then

less than I expected. I don't stash pills
because I don't want to die

Because.

I have only expectations of more loss
tossed and truncated telomeres

because my brain can't hold
the truth of his death in my two hands.

People tell me to hold him in my heart
but I want to throw the whole damned drama

to Asia or Alaska, to Zambia or Zanzibar
to the beginning or the end of everything

that defines a continent. I want to leave
the continent of grief.

No.
That is a lie.

I want to dwell on grief, in it
above it, to the right and the left of it

to inhabit the night, the dark and the light
swab the moon and swallow the sun.

I want them to stop
in their tracks. I want chicks

to crack their shells and kittens
to lick cyanide-laced milk.

I pound every detail of the day
into the truth of my loss —

pound every detail of loss into my truth
embracing our lost world and film noir.

I sink into the black themes
of Welles and Orwell and watch the ant

in the garden with his matchstick log. I watch him
climb the brick stairs like Sisyphus.

I push my own lumber, my own rock
like the ant, but with no end in sight, to no end.

Without

Without him, I am with the long line of widows
the color and shape of their wings fluttering.
I am the only one with me now.

With me, I am together with myself
in the long afternoon of grief.
With tears and keening.

With all the capes and shrouds that are necessary and lonely.
I am with blue, with lavender, with roses in the garden
though I am not with him.

And Him was the one I was with and now I'm without him
some days with a loneliness that I need a tent to contain
and other days with solitude that expands like bread rising.

I am with the bed and the pillows at night. I am with my dog
and she is with me and we are without him — with the night.
I am with the blackness of never and forever.

With is the eternal extrusion of his life with me
and our bed with dog, with open quilt, with loss, with
abstruse longing.

> Every with posits a without. Like his skin with its brown
> smoothness conjures Toni Morrison's child who says
> the white man is without skin.

> With shines in the together land of piano with keys, black and
> white, that open doors. Notes with flow. Notes within pages
> that speak as if they were alive.

> Polar bears live with ice, on ice. The ice melts
> and we are without polar bears. Drowning with dignity
> is an oxymoron — a pallid notion that flies from the mouths

Of the withs, the haves, the ones who don't understand
without or have not. With is a symbol of wealth,
a golden dream, a full moon, a bright sun.
With is the possibility of rain, of love.

With him I could hear and see and smell the textures of air.
With him I was the full moon. With him I was the wind
and the sea or a dolphin with the possibility of echo location.

With creates a world that is sonorous, harmonious,
rich and full and dark and round. With is not linear.
With is not dead.

Every with conjures a without, and the clairvoyant kiss knew
some day it would be without us, even though
we were with each other when our tongues entwined.

Now I am with her, the grieving widow. She is with me
and we are with every cold wind through the bamboo
that withers without water.

Mike's Papers

Mike's papers —I set them aside
like wishbones to dry.
Grief is not a concept
but the ring on my wedded finger
ashes in a bag
three bottles of shaving lotion
on the bathroom counter
a bereavement group.

I watched the bits of bone, the sooty mass
that was Mike
float away from the boat
forming a question mark amid rose petals
on the surface of the water.
I harbor all the questions
about how death expresses itself
in an urn or a box, in the dirt or the air,
on land or at sea.

Flesh burns at 140 degrees.
I must know this fact,
that transforms him to ashes
that I can hold in my two hands
and remember him before he was just dust
before he was hooked
to the breathing machine
before his lids closed like blankets
before he forgot how to breathe
and his heart sped up until it stopped
while I was trying to hold on to him,
and fluid was filling him up.

I began to smell death
in the room, but I held onto the taste
of our first kiss, and now

this last kiss was empty of taste
because I felt empty and he was full of liquid
and the nurse was fiddling with dials on machines
and adjusting tubes that stuck out of Mik'es mouth and nose
and hung off the edge of the bed, covered by blankets and sheets
even as his hands looked so soft on the quilt
even as I couldn't believe he was leaving,
and a haze hung over the room
until everything stopped.

The machines went silent.
The room became a tomb
which the nurse asked Michael and Donna and me to leave
after the priest's last rites, after our love chants
because someone was coming to wheel the cooling body
to the morgue. My hands were ice as the three of us left
and the nurse closed the door;
a woman in scrubs came after us and offered me
the quilt that had covered him —wrappped in a plastic bag —
and I took it, and I took his bag of clothes
and I took my coat and my gloves, and I forgot the
umbrella the taxi driver had given me, and I forgot the list of his clothes
but it didn't matter because I had his levis, his work shoes, his Ugg
slippers,
his Jockey underwear.
I didn't have him.

I have his papers.
I have ashes and bits of bone and teeth.
I have two black leather jackets.
I have his basement of sheet music and videos.
I have his collection of pie recipes and dishes.
I have his apron from Pike Place Market.
I have his trombones.
I have his music wafting up from the basement
I have the gigs: the bandstands and the Bowl and Central Avenue.
I have the cold sheets on his side of the bed.
I don't have him.

Grief Nonet

(Bass, Piano)
He is not dead
and I am not alone.
I can't read. I am surrounded
by the talismans of a life
I am surrounded by everything he is —
that I sit in his blue velvet chair
means that he is not dead. Or
there are feats and facts
beyond my knowing.

(Piano)
Juxtaposed to the empty space
where life languishes —
horses prance through their civilization —
all the dead dance. All the dead
in a ring of green light
wearing crowns of labradorite and sapphires.
All the dead come home to their loved ones
beneath the black holes of poverty and loss.
All the dead gathered on their planet.

(Bass, Piano, Trombone)
As in the year 3050.
Fallow or fallen or far away —
the "f" at the end of the word grief
just goes on and on and on
without any exclamation point, never ending
not like joy with its exclaimed end.
The resilient write home
even if home is a dead space between Kansas and Iowa
as large as the whole continent of grief.

(Cello, Bass)
I am not alone

between mouth and lip of glass
exists the possibility for dynamic intention.
If the vines are thick into Saturday night
If the grapes are ripe
from the heart of Napa-Sonoma-Mendocino
buried in a sea of gluttony: ripe olives arriving
abound, even as the distributors of polished books of the month
bring stories of courtship, fraught with memorized histories.

(Drums, Piano)
He is not dead.
Because.
I am not a widow
or a metronomed melody
from the censored vitality
of a jazz riff,
not an aberration of language
not sketches on a notepad
not diaphanous teachings of a nightdress.

(Cello, Bass, Drums, Saxophone)
If aberrations of language and Stephen King matter
if all the books are burned — as if that matters
now that Ray Bradbury is dead —35 and under don't read —
if biblical codes, if people (little spiritual diseases)
mark apocalyptic resonance
we are analogs of the suffering of the Left Ones
remnants of manatees and elephants
bones, dried leaves, a brown baseball hat.
I am a widow.

(Drums, Saxophone)
He is not dead
If Anne Sexton's dybbuk
the poet of strained glass
crashes into expository stress.
and Dr. Dre borrows cars to signify.

(Drumbeat. Drumbeat.)
He is dead.
My tribe sends signals through the air:
Hot wind. Hot music.

(Piano, Bass, Trombone)
If he is not dead, I am not a widow.
If the .com boxes are as seamless as music . . . .
In red shoes dancing, like barbeque,
Oliver Nelson and David Bowie
sing soliloquies that lift
a hydroponic garden of little vices —
paper doll, stick figure,
bag of soot, box of ashes —
a requiem for the end of time.

Friday Night Flamenco

Friday nights
used to be the best nights,
Mike's favorite nights
castanet nights, now the worst nights
with no exuberant Mike bouncing up the walk
even though the butterflies in the buddleia
continue to dance their dance, flit and twirl
in their unaware beauty
celebrating their wanton exuberance
because it is their season
and the season of the bush's purple flowers
with their myriad seeds bursting on the summer air
while I am bursting with all seven stages of grief
a dance all its own
a passionate one-step, alone-step, shoulda-been-a-two-step
all tears, all snot, all memory released against the window
with a sound loud enough to break glass.

If I had wings
I would beat them so hard
they would fall off. If I had antennae
I would search up and down
for Mike's dark eyes and skin.
I would pound every moment
into the question of his hair: Silver?
Or bald?
Does grief ever become a sweet hair-do
or is it always this dirty handkerchief
I want to stuff in a pocket or somebody's mouth
any mouth, so no one will ever say again
 "widow" or "dead" or "do" or "don't weep"
or "bouquet" or "covered dish"
so no one will ever want to sing hallelujah
or stomp a flamenco or slide a tango
so the world will stop its inevitable spin
and gravity will release all the dead
from the ash pile and the humus.

A butterfly will land on my hand
and turn from beauty to ghost to worm to Mike
rising up against me, right here in the garden
next to the buddleia, while the finches dip their beaks
in the fountain and bathe each other
to the syncopation of their wings. My man and I
will embrace each other on the earth
where the butterfly bush whips its grey-green leaves
against the sunset sky, and the future will not come.

The past will last and last and last
and our first kiss and our last kiss
will be the same kiss
and there will be no death and no birth
only the long ride on the wave of the eternal now.

SASSY FACTS

The Sassy Facts of Life

Nobody sends in the clowns better
than Sarah Vaughn
not Tom Jones, or Mel Tormé
not Judy Collins or Cleo Lane
not even Barbra Streisand.
There are seasons and reasons
to believe in clowns, and Sarah
makes me believe.

I used to attach to this song
because I was losing my marriage
to thin air. I could wallow,
a pining penitent, when Sarah
lost her, lost her, lost . . . lost
her timing so late in her career.
Like I was losing my youth
and my attraction to a man
who was losing his youth, but now

I think more about my timing,
about choosing a man
who would die before me,
and the fact is, both men are in
mid-air — all gravity lost —
and I face the grave myself.

The whole damned opera is conducted
by clowns who trick you into thinking
you'll be here for longer than you will
and maybe Wim Wenders has it all wrapped up
in *Wings of Desire*. The technicolor ride
is brief, and all the rest of eternity
is black and white.

Everywhere you turn, there are clowns

opening doors into empty spaces
where someone becomes no one
and the speed of light
is the fact of your life.

This Life, That Whore

Life's glued together
from sawdust and junipers
the detritus of a woman's love
or her misshapen hope.

An infant is either a blessing
or an accident
held between the poles
of the crucifix
and an icy mountain
that refuses to melt —
from his squalling entry
to his wailing death
he dreams of transformation
through his flower garden
or the limp diction of his politics.

He never makes it with this life —
that whore, that temptress
who tries with her vivid costumes
and rampant sensuality
to woo him. He never makes it
with her because his timidity
or his temerity keeps him
circling himself
like a 78 record
spinning in a stuck groove.

Fabric

Yards and yards of fabric —
florals, plaids, large and small prints,
stripes, denims and velvets, my sons' baby quilts
buttons from their shirts, sewn and outgrown
swatches cut from skirt linings and jacket sleeves—
all stacked by the chair where I sit,
opposite the writing side of my ancient oak partner's desk,
sewing through the night, sliding the presser foot across velvet and silk
cutting up the moiré skirt from one of my bridesmaid's dresses
stitching delicate bags for lingerie and jewelry,
gifts for friends and daughters-in-law, donations for an auction.

Unable to write
I turn to needle, thread and cloth
sewing, then sorting and resorting the stacks of fabric
and watching the haze of dawn
stretch its way across the wooden desk
as I hand-stitch lace to silk
instead of inking words on linen
failing even to imagine how to spin a story or a poem
from a few cryptic lines borrowed from the writer I admire most today,
whom I will grow to envy, then hate.

As morning breaks
I dust off the writing side
of the desk and move toward the impossible
dive into my watery underworld
where seaweed gives birth to itself
over and over, and shark egg cases float
until they wash up on shore
empty and dry, like the sky after a storm
as the words fold up in my mouth.

I move back to the other side of the desk
giving my weight to the foot pedal

and turn the wheel to stitch a silken bag
that will hold some of my art and all of my shame.

The ACLU Comes Home

I stand at the stove, stirring oatmeal and reading ads
for liposuction and colonics and start to wonder
about the shape of *my* colon
if it's a smooth subway tube
or a cobra in the basket of my belly.
But I'm afraid it's a twisted, contorted tunnel
like the one in the ad, afraid I've become
my dead ex-mother-in-law
padding down a dark hall in *Dearfoam* slippers
worrying about my bowels
when I could be daydreaming
about Clarence Darrow's heroism
in the defense of blacks and kids and underdogs
or thanking Roger Baldwin, precursor to the ACLU
for defending the Jehovah's Witnesses' free press rights
for backing John Scopes and getting the ban lifted
from Joyce's *Ulysses*. I could be reading that.

I could be outside. I could pick up dog shit
between rainstorms, or I could have continued
to let the waves batter me against the cliff
early this morning, while the dog scurried to high ground.
I could, could, could stop
stirring the cereal and dish it up.
But I continue twirling my spoon through the sacred mush
when two blond Jehovah's Witnesses
in grey suits knock on the door,
which I answer and tell them I am catholic
so they'll leave. I go back to the oatmeal
which is starting to get hard.

At the stove again, I begin to sort Baldwins:
that mediocre actor, Alec, then a string of kings of Jerusalem
(especially the twelfth century child-king who died of leprosy)
and I think of James M. Baldwin who applied Darwin's theories

to psychology, then James A., writing on a mountaintop.
I wonder if he and Roger Baldwin ever met
and who among them all might have loved
Molly Bloom or Aimee Semple McPherson
who died her foursquare death
when she was only fifty-three,
like Molly reportedly having gone wild
about the body thing. I knew so little about it myself
when the necessary perpendicularity
of a penis first pushed at my thigh
and my nipple hardened in a boy's mouth
as we tumbled like weeds in the dunes.

Standing at the stove
I stir the years through the mush
a blend of scatology and eschatology
as the whiskered face of my friend's eccentric Irish step-father
hovers over the oatmeal. (He taught me *quip*, for my Scrabble *q*.)
and again above the toaster-oven where he defrosts a blackberry pie
while his Dachshund, Fyodor Dostoevsky
and the mutt, Dulcinea Popgut,
locked together at their loins, roil by our feet.
He makes a raunchy joke about the "bloody" pie and calls me
Aimee Semple McTeenager to my naive face
as he scoops the pie onto our plates.

Transient as steam, Aimee and Molly,
Michael Daly and his dogs,
the Baldwins and Darwin
even today's Jehovah's Witness proselytizers
hang in the air while my burnt mush sticks to the pan.
I scrape some into a bowl with yogurt
apple chunks and walnuts.
I eat.

Morning Sarcophagus

A subversive pattern of light
accompanied by shadows
leads morning into my bedroom.
From the red and black calligraphy painting
on top of the kiri wood tansu chest
to the streak of light across the far wall
and the day is aloft, while I am adrift
with the brightening air signaling me to assemble
the disparate parts of myself that have traveled
in separate bodies all night long.

My feet have wound up and down Sierra trails with my father
wandered the coral reef behind my mother's Hawaiian home
while I watched her swimming with her dog
and my body that was nestled into Phil's or Mike's
comes back to me when I open my ears
to the fountain's trickle outside the window.

I return to my sea-green room
and arrange my dead intimates
into an ornate sarcophagus in a corner
of my psychic acreage,
make peace with their spirits
move them from the dreamworld
into this wooden box where I store them every day
then pull the covers off, put on my robe
and stand before the gleaming, stainless kitchen
where the disparate parts of myself coalesce
in the harsh evanescence of morning.

I mix two deep reds
of a pomegranate and cranberry elixir
and laugh at the self that gets such joy
from this blessed juice,
as though standing here in my kitchen

I am sipping the blood of the savior
so I will be healed
and all my Dead will come back
for the diaphanous do-over of my dreams.

Grief Maze

Grief screams, begs to be a pal, a dog, a best pet.
She doesn't purr or growl. She glues herself
to my gut, chants in my shoes
raves in my hair. She's the brutal animal
that breaks her leash and wears no collar.

She has a particular destination,
pushes into the hub of my existence.
She won't play yahtzee or tidily-winks
and she's never as benign as a maze
with dead ends that beat me to my own thoughts.

No, she rambles. She churns.
She buries me alive with heavy baskets
of tears and broken soliloquies
about bodies and the prospect of love
about storms and thrashing dreams

About rhyme and begonias with flame-tossed leaves.
Grief is a mendicant, two-timing wanna-be.
She's not a highway but the vehicle itself
churning me toward the dead end
of my slippery, mortal landscape.

I'm afraid of her tenses — past, future,
present or perfect, because all of them
are the homeland of this specter,
this dyspeptic ghost, this glee-filled witch,
a phenomenon waiting for the earth to collide
with the next darkest planet
expunged from God's realm.

There's no end in sight for the salt rivers
that ooze from my eyes, not only
for my failed kidneys, or the man who left me

bereft and crying, not only for him
and for me and for us,
but for detusked elephants, species demise
myriad planetary losses and intergalactic crashes.

Meeting Summer

All my hungers hang like open overcoats.
The cactus have drunk unsparingly of the wet
and cottonwoods have unfurled again.

The dry days begin to stretch across the longest season
when the light eats at me
and the rattlesnake slides out of her skin.
No transition.
Bare moments rarely arrive outside their season.
Gifts come unexpected, despite
rigid floral predictions that autumn will arrive
in its usual discreet way, on top of flat, hot sand.

Coyotes sing their parched, evening song.
I taste the night's darkness; it's as thick as the warm tears
a widow mourns onto bones that settle into their grave.

I feel earth shift beneath sand
and understand the risk desert velvet takes
when it plants itself between agave and a rock; still
there is enough moisture to push a sacred dream toward god.

WEEPING AND LAUGHTER

Grace Unknown

Disjointed wilderness
my mind.
It spins a future
out of a past
elevates the pieces
to myth.

My life will never be
as large
as sunflowers
tall enough to shed seeds
at the feet
of the gods.

My life will never be
a hundred yellow roses
piles of lavender
or leucodendron reaching
toward bees and dragonflies
in the garden
that I planted
as a hedge against
the brown wilderness
of the grief that grows
where joy once lived.

Hope. Future.
They've run away
leaving only dirty footprints
the wide nothing
and the narrow something
that lie outside my garden
when the gate swings open
on its rusty hinges.
Grace is an elusive guardian.

Children, Legs

Built on the flotsam of childhood
                    my life.
I can't imagine a different way
        only different debris.
My specifics   iodine-stained knees
        wicked witch of the west
                        a lost arrangement of
                        I'm through with Love.

        Salt dries on my cheeks
for the failure to remember
which pedal to press
for sustain.

        My legs lose any memory of shape
in long, grey skirts
opaque stockings of yesteryear.
I cloak my breasts in vests and scarves
and the shame of age.

                I don't go bare-armed
                or cut bougainvillea
        with its blood red stain of leaf
but eat the early-bird special   a turkey sandwich
        cranberry sauce   gravy from a bowl.

                I squawk and cry
                over the days when
my legs and my children were young
beg them both to support me now
        symptom and symbol of declension

                that only the sharpest love might touch.

Grabbing Grunion

I haven't grabbed a grunion
in over fifty years.
In fifty years, I haven't grabbed a grunion
or chewed small bones after frying
I haven't eaten one, fried like a trout.
I haven't eaten a trout that way either
straight out of the river
in nearly as long,
as long as it takes to forget about
my hands grabbing a grunion
or a cock.

I haven't grabbed a cock in a decade.
I long. I look. In my sleep
I grab, but there is no fish —
no trout, no grunion
no cock.

I would like to reach out across
the chasm of the bed
and grab his cock.
I would just hold on.
I don't even think about it in my pussy
or my mouth, just holding on
and dreaming of the grunion and the trout
dreaming of grabbing any thing that is alive
and hanging on

and swinging the handle of the silver bucket
and grabbing the grunion
and eating it whole
because that's what kids do
because it doesn't matter
about the bones.

It just matters that you can grab on
that you are free
because you can taste, and when you're old
you just dream of the thing
remember the thing
don't really have the thing.

Fifty years is a long time
to hold a memory — of any thing
of the bucket that held the sea water
and the silvery fish —
of the sand and the moon
of the friend with the curly brush-up hair
and the built-in bunks
and the mother who fried the tiny fish
and I wish I were grabbing grunion
singing a fishy song, a hymn to the bony blessing
of the fish and the night and the stars,
a bony blessing to my friend, Sharon
who called last week
to see how I was. A bony blessing.

Fifty years is a long time
and she still cares
and we haven't grabbed grunion
in over fifty years
and her husband is dead.
I introduced them. We rode
in his green boat car,
a Nash
and fifty years is a long time
to know a friend, and now I know
she doesn't really know me any more
any more than I know her
because we've moved with the tide and the moon.

The silver fish are still sliding

in and out of the sea,
still swimming, still spawning, still growing
on so many nights that I've not fished.
My youth, my deft hands,
the silver bucket
my friend,
the grunion, the trout, the cock —
it's all sliding
into a sea on a far away beach
because I am growing old,
growing closer to still.

Desert Footnote

The desert remembers
blood and bodyprints
buried in sand.

The wind covers
your shadow
in a shallow grave

And the rattlesnake twists
a path across the flat land.

Yucca blooms.

A Thunder of Swans

Forget about masks. Forget about cracked eggs
on your mother's kitchen floor. Forget about fear.
Live in the wild elements, no matter how hostile they seem.

Be the woman who cries out in the open field
the man who carries his losses on his lips.
Be a crack of thunder. Re-member yourself.

> Become both expert and novice
> speaking the eloquent language
> of body, full as a summer-red grape
> fleshing into the sky, because
> you are riding this horse of your life
> all the way to the end.

Forget about appearance and disappearance. Forget everything
you ever learned about being small
because the ride offers inevitable gifts. Fighting against the end
even against the earth's melting at its poles
is a grand waste of time. So flow toward unknown dimensions
toward an immense energy field of loss and abundance

Where there are no questions and no answers
only weeping and laughter, laughter and weeping
the sole anodynes in the end. So fly
like a thunder of swans. Shake and shimmer
in the excruciating joy
of your exquisitely bearable, temporary life.

CLOUD LIFE

Cloud Life

I am here
on a temporary assignment
that I keep trying
to make permanent

while clouds

                shadow

across a ceaseless sky

          forming
and reforming

I never expected
to be like a cloud
          myself

          skinny
then full
then
                    gone

"Me here at last on the ground,
you in mid-air."

–Stephen Sondheim
"Send In The Clowns"